Literacy Line-Up

PERSONAL WRITING

Written and compiled by

David Orme

Contents

From

Cider With Rosie

In this extract from his autobiography Laurie Lee describes his first day at school.

The morning came, without any warning, when my sisters surrounded me, wrapped me in scarves, tied up my boot-laces, thrust a cap on my head, and stuffed a baked potato in my pocket.

'What's this?' I said.

'You're starting school today.'

'I ain't. I'm stopping 'ome.'

'Now, come on, Loll. You're a big boy now.'

'I ain't.'

'You are.'

'Boo-hoo.'

They picked me up bodily, kicking and bawling, and carried me up to the road.

'Boys who don't go to school get put into boxes, and turn into rabbits, and get chopped up Sundays.'

I felt this was overdoing it rather, but I said no more after that. I arrived at the school just three feet tall and fatly wrapped in my scarves. The playground roared like a rodeo, and the potato burned through my thigh. Old boots, ragged stockings, torn trousers and skirts, went skating and skidding around me.

The rabble closed in: was encircled; grit flew in my face like shrapnel. Tall girls with frizzed hair, and huge boys with sharp elbows, began to prod me with hideous interest. They plucked at my scarves, spun me round like a top, screwed my nose, and stole my potato.

I was rescued at last by a gracious lady -
the sixteen-year-old junior teacher, who
boxed a few ears and dried my face and
led me off to The Infants. I spent that
first day picking holes in paper, then
went home in a smouldering
temper.

'What's the matter, Loll? Didn't he like it at school then?'

'They never gave me the present!'

'Present? What present?'

'They said they'd give me a present.'

'Well, now, I'm sure they didn't.'

'They did! They said: "You're Laurie Lee, ain't you? Well, just you sit there for the present." I sat there all day but I never got it. I ain't going back there again!'

Let me persuade you!

Why I like living in a city!

My name is Sanjay and I live in a big city. I think cities are great and I wouldn't want to live anywhere else.

1 Cities are better for the environment. People think cities are smelly, dirty, places, so they're surprised when I say this, but here are my reasons.

•The countryside is being destroyed by more and more houses. In cities, more people can live in less space; their home might be in blocks of flats, for example.

•Because everything you need is very close it is easier to walk there – you do not need to use your car for every journey.

2   It's easier to make friends in the city. There are many more people around so you're bound to find plenty of really good friends! I would soon get lonely if there were nothing but cows and sheep for miles and miles!

3 If you want to travel to the seaside or other towns, or even abroad, it's much easier if you live in a city because stations and airports are close by. If you live in the country you have to travel to the city first before you can even start your journey.

4 Parks are much better than the countryside. There are no farmers complaining about you leaving gates open, or dangerous animals roaming about.

5 Things are much cheaper to buy in the city, because there are so many big stores all competing with each other. If you live in the country, where could you go to buy things like designer clothes? You would go to the city, of course!

6   There is so much to do in the city! Whatever you are interested in, there will be something for you in the city. Here is a list of some of the places you can go to.

Museums

Musical events

Sporting events like football matches

Swimming pools and recreation centres

Historical buildings

Shopping malls

Libraries

Clubs

Places where you can try many different types of food.

Now you have read this I am sure you agree with me that, although the countryside can be beautiful (if you like fields and trees), the city is the best place to live!

Letter from Mrs Stevenson

This letter was written by the wife of
Robert Louis Stevenson. She describes a journey they
made in the Pacific Ocean.

My Dear Friend,

Louis has improved so wonderfully in the delicious islands of the South Seas, that we are thinking of one more voyage. You could hardly believe it if you could see Louis now. He looks as well as he ever did in his life.

As for myself, I have had more cares than I was really fit for. To keep house on a yacht is no easy thing. When Louis and I broke loose from the ship and lived alone amongst the natives I got on very well. It was when I was deathly sea-sick, and the question was put to me by the cook, 'What shall we have

for the cabin dinner, what for
tomorrow's breakfast, what for lunch?
And what about the sailors' food?
Please come and look at the biscuits, for
the weevils have got into them, and
show me how to make yeast that will
rise of itself and smell the pork which
seems pretty high, and give me
directions about making a pudding with
molasses – and what is to be done
about the bugs?' etc. etc.

In the midst of heavy dangerous weather, when I was lying on the floor clutching a basin, down comes the mate with a cracked head, and I must needs cut off the hair matted with blood, wash and dress the wound, and administer restoratives. I do not like being the 'Lady of the yacht', but ashore! Oh, then I felt I was repaid for all.

Fanny Stevenson

TWO DIARIES

The two diary extracts describe destruction of part of London by fire. The first comes from the diary of Samuel Pepys and describes the Great Fire of London in 1666. The second describes the Blitz in the Second World War.

Sunday September 2nd 1666

*S*ome of our maids who were sitting up late called us at about three in the morning, to tell us of a great fire they saw in the city. So I went to the window, and, not being used to such fires, thought that it was far enough away and so went to bed again.

Soon Jane came and told me that she had heard that more than 300 houses had been burned down last night, and that the fire is now burning down all Fish street by London Bridge.

I went down to the waterside, and there got a boat and went through London Bridge.

There I saw the terrible fire. Everyone was trying to save their belongings, by flinging them into the river or carrying them into barges. Poor people were staying in their houses until the fire reached them, then ran into the boats, or clambered from one pair of stairs by the waterside to another. Amongst other things, I noticed that the poor pigeons were unwilling to leave their houses, so they hovered by the windows and balconies until some of them burnt their wings and fell down.

Diary of
Samuel Pepys

Sunday, 18 August 1940

We had just settled down to a delightful dinner – chicken, peas, new potatoes and baked potatoes, stuffing and gravy, when the air-raid sirens started. Dad and Alan both took their dinners down the shelter. I, only dressed in pants and singlet, took some four minutes to dress, and, hugging my briefcase, I too toddled off down.

Aircraft were roaring overhead, and I didn't have time to survey the scene. However, having deposited my belongings safely below ground, I came up to the surface. I went across to No. 1 block to the top floor, and sure enough, Croydon once again was in smoke.

A big fire also showed in the Wimbledon direction. Putney, too, appeared to have been hit, but it may have been a factory chimney. As I was looking out I heard a terrific roar approaching, and being from the north I could not see anything from where I stood, so I ran into the court, to the shelter, where everyone was busily scanning the sky.

Then I shouted – first again – some 30 or 40 enemy bombers, accompanied by fighters, were sweeping in a direct line for Croydon. They were indeed very near us. It presented an amazing spectacle, like a swarm of bees surrounding their queen; fascinating, most certainly.

A puff of smoke and the sound of a gun signalled our retreat down the shelter. I fancied I heard the whine of dive-bombers, most assuredly we heard the guns and crunch of falling bombs. I imagined this was the real commencement of hostilities against the British Isles.

After a few moments I again came up; I

wanted to stay in the flat all the time, but for the sake of my parents I went down. Davis tried to keep me down, but my answer to him, if he tries again, is that I am eighteen years of age, old enough for military service and to fight and die for my country. Fellows only a year my senior are up there shooting the raiders down, and within a year I too hope to be there. That is good enough for him.

I popped indoors and finished off my dinner, and went once again to the top floor, but the smoke had cleared, and nothing was to be seen. Evidently not a great deal of really substantial damage had been done. The 'all clear' sounded soon after, and we went back to cold chicken. Damn, the only time for months we have had a chicken and then the Nazis have to spoil it.

Diary of Colin Perry